Mermaid COOKBOOK

Barbara Beery

Gibbs Smith, Publisher

TO ENRICH AND INSPIRE HUMANKIND

Salt Lake City | Charleston | Santa Fe | Santa Barbara

First Edition
12 11 10 09 08 15 14 13 12 11 10 9 8 7 6 5 4 3 2 1

Text © 2008 Barbara Beery
Photographs © 2008 Kirsten Shultz
Food styling by Susan Massey
Cover photograph © 2008 Zachary Williams
Cover food styling by Jennifer Grillone

Published by
Gibbs Smith, Publisher
P.O. Box 667
Layton, Utah 84041

Orders: 1.800.835.4993
www.gibbs-smith.com
www.kidscookingshop.com
www.batterupkids.com
Designed by Dawn DeVries Sokol
Printed and bound in China

Library of Congress Cataloging-in-Publication Data
Beery, Barbara, 1954-
   Mermaid cookbook / Barbara Beery ; photographs by Kirsten Shultz ; cover
photograph by Zachary Williams. — 1st ed.
       p. cm.
   ISBN-13: 978-1-4236-0417-4
   ISBN-10: 1-4236-0417-2
   1. Cookery—Juvenile literature. 2. Mermaids in art—Juvenile literature.
I. Title.

TX652.5.B366 2008
641.5—dc22

                    2007047596

Contents

Fruits de Mermaid

Seaside Fruit Soup 4
Coconut Fruit Sorbet 7
Mermaid Bay Baked Bananas 8
Paradise Pineapple Fruit Dip 11
Fruit Salsa 12

Seaside Sipping

Sea Foam Floats 14
Lemonade Lagoon Coolers 15
Swirling Mermaid Smoothies 17
Cool Breeze Slushies 18
Under a Blue Moon Milkshake 21

Crunchy Sea Snacks

Treasure Island Trail Mix 22
Golden Cheese Doubloons 25
Goldfish Gorp 26
Sea Crunch Bagel Crisps 29

Small Bites

Maiden Mermaid Salad 30
Weeki Wachee Roll-Ups 33
Sweet Seaweed Slaw 34
Triton's Tuna Fish Sandwiches 37

Cookies and Cakes

Starfish Cookies 39
Sea Turtle Cookies 43
Little Luau Cakes 44
Sand Dollars 47
Hidden Treasure Cupcakes 48

Sweet Mermaid Treats

Tiki Hut Fruit Tarts 51
Sea Queen Kabobs 53
Water Fairy Ice Pops 55
Banana Split Boats 56
Rainbow Fish Fudge 59
Seashell Candy 60
Sea Maiden Sand Cups 63

Seaside Fruit Soup

Ingredients List

1 cup nonfat vanilla yogurt

2 tablespoons fresh squeezed orange juice

1 cup sliced fresh strawberries

1 to 2 tablespoons honey

Tiny pinch ground black pepper

½ cup raspberries

½ cup blueberries

1 kiwifruit, sliced

Extra fruit for garnish

Makes 4 servings

Let's get whirling!

Mix all ingredients together in a food processor or blender. Store in a covered container in the refrigerator for up to 8 hours.

To serve, pour equally into 4 cups or bowls and garnish with extra fruit.

Smooth and sweet!

Coconut Fruit Sorbet

Ingredients List

1 (15-ounce) can Coco Lopez brand cream of coconut

⅓ cup fresh lime juice

¾ cup water

¼ teaspoon ground ginger

¼ teaspoon almond extract

2 fresh coconuts, drained, and cracked in half

½ cup toasted coconut

1 mango, sliced and chopped into small cubes

4 fresh raspberries

Makes 4 servings

Let's get freezing!

Combine cream of coconut, lime juice, water, ginger, and almond extract in a mixing bowl with a whisk.

Pour into an electric ice cream maker and freeze according to manufacturer's directions.

Divide sorbet equally among the coconut shell halves and garnish with toasted coconut, chopped mango, and raspberries.

You'll go coco-loco with this tropical treat!

Mermaid Bay Baked Bananas

Ingredients List

2 cups crushed corn flakes

1 teaspoon cinnamon

4 slightly green bananas, peeled and cut in half lengthwise

2 to 3 tablespoons honey

Frozen vanilla yogurt (optional)

Assorted fresh berries (optional)

¼ cup powdered sugar (optional)

Makes 6-8 servings

Enjoy your baked bananas down by the bay!

Let's get crushing!

Preheat oven to 350 degrees F. Line a cookie sheet with foil and spray with nonstick cooking spray. Set aside.

Pour corn flakes and cinnamon into a ziplock bag and seal shut. Put bag in another ziplock bag and seal shut. Crush mixture with your hands. Set aside.

Place bananas on prepared cookie sheet. With a small spatula or pastry brush, coat each banana half with honey on all sides.

Using a fork, pick up a banana slice and put it into the ziplock bag with the corn flake mixture. Seal bag shut and shake to coat. Place coated banana back onto cookie sheet. Repeat until all banana slices have been coated. Sprinkle any leftover corn flake mixture evenly over the tops of bananas.

Bake for 10 minutes; remove from oven. Garnish warm bananas with frozen yogurt, berries, and powdered sugar, if desired. Serve immediately.

Paradise Pineapple Fruit Dip

Ingredients List

1 (8-ounce) package cream cheese, softened

1 cup nonfat strawberry yogurt

¼ cup honey

1 teaspoon vanilla extract

1 (8-ounce) can crushed pineapple, drained

Makes approximately 3 cups

Let's get mixing!

With an electric mixer in a medium-sized bowl, beat cream cheese, yogurt, honey, and vanilla until light and fluffy. Fold in pineapple.

Store covered in refrigerator for up to 8 hours.

Serve with Sea Crunch Bagel Crisps (see page 29), baby carrots, and celery sticks.

A bite of paradise in every dip!

Fruit Salsa

Ingredients List

2 kiwifruit, peeled and diced

2 Golden Delicious apples, cored and diced

1 cup raspberries

1 cup blueberries

2 cups chopped strawberries

1 cup dried cranberries

3 tablespoons strawberry preserves

1 teaspoon lime zest

Makes 8-10 servings

Let's get stirring!

Combine all ingredients in a large mixing bowl. Cover and refrigerate until ready to serve.

Great served with animal crackers, graham crackers, or vanilla wafers.

A sensational salsa snack!

Sea Foam Floats

Ingredients List

1 liter lemon-lime soda, chilled

1 pint raspberry or lemon sherbet

1 can whipped cream topping

Fresh raspberries

Makes 8 servings

Let's get floating!

Pour lemon-lime soda into 8 glasses, filling each about three-fourths full. Place 2 scoops sherbet in each glass of soda.

Garnish with whipped cream topping and fresh raspberries. Serve immediately.

Float away to sweet dreams!

Lemonade Lagoon Coolers

Ingredients List

6 lemons, juiced

½ cup sugar

2 quarts apple juice, chilled

Pineapple chunks for garnish

Strawberry slices for garnish

Apple slices for garnish

Makes 8-10 servings

Cool down with
these coolers!

Let's get squeezing!

In a large pitcher or punch bowl, combine lemon juice and sugar. Stir until sugar has completely dissolved.

Add apple juice. Stir in 2 to 4 cups of ice and garnish with fruit as desired. Serve immediately.

Swirling Mermaid Smoothies

Ingredients List

CHERRY

½ cup vanilla yogurt

½ banana

½ cup vanilla soy milk

1 cup pitted fresh cherries
(frozen may be used)

ORANGE

½ cup vanilla yogurt

½ banana

½ cup vanilla soy milk

½ cup fresh squeezed
orange juice

Makes 3-4 servings

Let's get whirling!

For the cherry smoothie, mix vanilla yogurt, banana, and milk in a blender. Add the cherries and blend on low speed for 30 seconds. Pour smoothie into a small pitcher or pour-spout measuring cup and place in freezer. Rinse out blender and dry.

For the orange smoothie, place all ingredients in blender and blend on low speed for 30 seconds. Pour smoothie into a small pitcher or pour-spout measuring cup.

Pour both smoothies into tall serving glasses at the same time to make them swirl. Serve immediately.

A swirly drink that's pretty and pink!

Cool Breeze Slushies

Ingredients List

3 cups fresh watermelon cubes

1 cup crushed ice

4 teaspoons lime juice

1 cup raspberry sorbet

Granny Smith apple cubes for
garnish

Makes 4 servings

Let's get slushing!

In a blender, combine watermelon, ice,
and lime juice. Add raspberry sorbet by
the spoonful and blend until smooth.

Divide mixture equally between glass
punch cups or glasses.

Garnish with fruit and serve immediately.

Fresh as a cool breeze!

Under a Blue Moon Milkshake

Ingredients List

2½ cups frozen blueberries

1¼ cups apple juice or white grape juice

1 cup vanilla frozen yogurt

¼ cup milk

½ teaspoon almond extract

½ teaspoon cinnamon

½ cup fresh blueberries for garnish

Makes 2 servings

Let's get shaking!

Combine all ingredients except berries for garnish in a blender. Serve immediately garnished with fresh blueberries.

Variation: Try using raspberries instead of blueberries.

Enjoy this shake more than once in a blue moon!

Treasure Island Trail Mix

Ingredients List

¼ cup macadamia nuts

¼ cup roasted soy nuts

¼ cup pretzel sticks

¼ cup each dried pineapple chunks, dried mango, and dried cherries

¼ cup dried banana chips

¼ cup white chocolate chips

Makes 2 cups

Let's get shaking!

Pour all ingredients into a large ziplock bag. Seal and shake.

Store sealed until ready to eat.

A tasty treasure!

Golden Cheese Doubloons

Ingredients List

2 cups grated cheddar cheese

1 cup butter, softened

2 cups flour

2 cups crispy rice cereal

½ teaspoon salt

½ teaspoon Worcestershire sauce

¼ teaspoon garlic powder

¼ teaspoon cayenne pepper

¼ teaspoon black pepper

2 tablespoons milk

2 tablespoons sesame or poppy seeds

Makes 25-30 crackers

Worth their weight in gold!

Let's get mixing!

Preheat oven to 350 degrees F. Line two cookie sheets with foil and spray with non-stick cooking spray. Set aside.

In a large bowl, combine cheese, butter, flour, cereal, salt, Worcestershire sauce, garlic powder, cayenne pepper, and black pepper.

Mix well with clean hands and form dough into small ½-inch balls.

Place dough balls 1 inch apart on prepared cookie sheets. Flatten out each ball with your fingertips.

Lightly brush the top of each flattened ball with milk and sprinkle evenly with sesame or poppy seeds.

Bake for 10 to 12 minutes, or until very lightly browned around the outer edges. Carefully put on a cooling rack to cool. Store covered for up to two days or freeze for up to one month.

Goldfish Gorp

Ingredients List

1 (6.6-ounce) package multi-colored Goldfish crackers

1 (12-ounce) bag mixed jumbo raisins

1 cup honey roasted peanuts

Makes 2 ½ cups

Let's get shaking!

Combine all ingredients in a large ziplock bag. Seal and shake.

Store sealed until ready to serve.

A colorful crunchy goldfish snack!

Sea Crunch Bagel Crisps

Ingredients List

6 mini bagels

½ cup colored sugar

1 teaspoon cinnamon

1 tablespoon butter, softened

Makes 24 crisps

Fancy sugar-and-cinnamon crisps!

Let's get sprinkling!

Preheat oven to 325 degrees F. Line a cookie sheet with foil and spray with nonstick cooking spray. Set aside.

Have an adult assistant help you slice the bagels in half, and then slice each piece in half again to make thin circles.

Combine sugar and cinnamon in a measuring cup. Stir to blend. Set aside.

With a small spatula or pastry brush, coat one side of each bagel slice with butter and sprinkle evenly with sugar mixture.

Place bagel slices on prepared cookie sheet and bake for 15 to 20 minutes, or until lightly browned. Remove from oven. Cool on pan for 5 minutes. Remove from pan and place on cooling rack for 10 minutes. The chips will become crispier as they cool.

When completely cooled, store in an airtight container for up to 2 days.

Maiden Mermaid Salad

Ingredients List

NOODLES

1 (3-ounce) package oriental-flavored ramen noodles

½ cup chopped celery

½ cup grated carrots

1 chopped green onion

½ cup chopped red, yellow, or orange bell pepper

½ cup snow peas

1 cup cooked shredded chicken breast

Let's get tossing!

Cook and drain ramen noodles according to package directions; then cool. Reserve seasoning packet for dressing.

For dressing, whisk together ramen seasoning, orange juice, soy sauce, and honey in a small bowl. Add mayonnaise and whisk again until creamy and smooth.

In a large bowl, toss together vegetables, chicken, and dressing.

Add noodles and gently mix. Cover and chill at least 1 hour before serving.

A salad extraordinaire!

DRESSING

Seasoning packet from ramen
   noodles

1 tablespoon fresh squeezed
   orange juice

2 teaspoons soy sauce

1 teaspoon honey

1 to 2 tablespoons mayonnaise

Makes 4 servings

Weeki Wachee Roll-Ups

Ingredients List

½ cup cream cheese, softened

½ teaspoon dried chives

4 (10-inch) whole wheat
   tortillas

½ cup hummus

1 cup shredded carrots

½ cup sprouts

½ cup sliced cherry tomatoes

4 leaves romaine lettuce,
   thinly sliced

½ cup crumbled feta or grated
   mozzarella cheese

Makes 4–6 servings

Let's get mixing!

In a small bowl, combine cream cheese and chives. Using a small spatula, spread the cream cheese mixture evenly over each tortilla within about 1 inch of the edge.

Spread a thin layer of hummus over the cream cheese. Layer carrots, sprouts, tomatoes, and lettuce and then sprinkle with cheese. Carefully roll up each tortilla.

Wrap each tortilla roll tightly in plastic wrap and chill for at least 30 minutes, or until ready to serve.

To serve, slice each roll into 3 pieces.

Wacky and wild!

Sweet Seaweed Slaw

Ingredients List

½ cup cider vinegar

2 tablespoons brown sugar

2 teaspoons poppy seeds

½ teaspoon salt

¼ teaspoon black pepper

2 cups thinly sliced Granny
  Smith apples

1 cup thinly sliced pear

1 (12-ounce) package
  cabbage-and-carrot coleslaw

Makes 6–8 servings

Let's get mixing!

In a small bowl, combine the first five ingredients with a whisk. Set aside.

In a large bowl, combine apples, pears, and coleslaw; stir in dressing. Cover and chill for at least 1 hour before serving.

Down by the sea and as sweet as can be!

Triton's Tuna Fish Sandwiches

Ingredients List

½ cup plain low-fat yogurt

2 tablespoons mayonnaise

2 teaspoons bottled basil pesto

1 large rib celery, diced

1 small red bell pepper, diced

1 small carrot, peeled and diced

½ cup packed spinach leaves, stems removed, thinly sliced

1 (6-ounce) can solid white water-packed tuna, drained

½ teaspoon salt

Pepper to taste

Whole wheat bread slices

Let's get spreading!

Place yogurt, mayonnaise, and basil pesto in a medium mixing bowl. Whisk to blend ingredients into a creamy dressing.

Add the celery, bell pepper, carrot, spinach, and tuna. Toss ingredients with dressing to coat.

Cover and store in refrigerator for up to 1 day.

Make into sandwiches by cutting the bread with cookie cutters into the shapes of fish or starfish. Spread the tuna mixture on one side of a cutout piece of bread. Place another slice of the same shape over tuna mixture and then spread more tuna

continued

Olives, cherry tomatoes, or
tiny pickles for garnish

Makes 4–6 servings

mixture on top. Place one more slice of the same shape bread over top for a tiny stacked sandwich.

To garnish the sandwich, stick top layer of bread with a toothpick skewered with a olive, tomato, or tiny pickle.

A royal sandwich!

Starfish Cookies

Ingredients List

COOKIES

½ cup butter, softened

¾ cup sugar

1 egg

¾ teaspoon vanilla extract

2 cups flour

½ teaspoon baking soda

½ teaspoon salt

Let's get baking!

Preheat oven to 375 degrees F. Line two cookie sheets with foil and spray with non-stick cooking spray. Set aside.

Cream butter in a large mixing bowl with a hand mixer. Add sugar, beating until light and fluffy. Add egg and vanilla, mixing well.

Combine flour, baking soda, and salt in a separate bowl. Add to creamed mixture, blending well. Dough will be very stiff.

Divide dough into thirds. Roll each portion to 1/8 inch thickness on lightly floured waxed paper. Cut out with star-shaped cookie cutters. Place cookies 2 inches apart on prepared cookie sheets.

Bake for 8 to 10 minutes, or until very slightly browned. Remove from oven and cool on pan for 5 minutes. Remove from pan and cool on wire racks for 15 minutes before frosting.

continued

FROSTING

3 tablespoons meringue
    powder

2 cups powdered sugar

¼ cup plus 2 tablespoons
    warm water

1 teaspoon vanilla extract

½ teaspoon almond extract

Assorted food coloring

Assorted candy decorations
    and sprinkles

Makes 3-4 dozen,
depending on the size of
the cookies

Let's get frosting!

Combine meringue powder, powdered sugar, water, and vanilla and almond extracts in a mixing bowl.

Beat on high speed with an electric mixer for 3 to 4 minutes.

Divide frosting evenly in several small bowls and stir in drops of food coloring as desired.

Frost and decorate cookies, then move them to a wire rack to dry completely (about 30 minutes). Store in a covered container until ready to use.

The "star" of any party!

Sea Turtle Cookies

Ingredients List

1½ cups pecan halves

24 caramels, unwrapped

1 cup milk chocolate chips, melted according to package directions

Assorted candy decorations

Makes 24 cookies

Eat one before it swims away!

Let's get melting!

Preheat oven to 325 degrees F. Line a cookie sheet with foil and spray with nonstick cooking spray. Set aside.

Break pecan halves into 5 thin pieces lengthwise to create 4 legs and a tail for each sea turtle cookie. Use one pecan half as the head of the sea turtle.

Arrange thin pecan slices, flat side down, on prepared cookie sheet, in clusters of 5 to form the turtle's four legs and tail. Place the pecan half for the head.

Put a caramel on top of each group of pecans. Place cookie sheet in oven and heat until caramels soften, about 5 minutes.

Cool cookies on pan for 10 minutes. Spoon about ½ teaspoon of melted chocolate onto each turtle and sprinkle with assorted candy decorations. Place in refrigerator to chill for 15 minutes and serve.

Little Luau Cakes

Ingredients List

1 frozen family-size pound cake

2 purchased containers
   vanilla frosting

Assorted gel food coloring

Assorted sprinkles, sugars,
   and candy decorations

Makes 24 mini cakes

Let's get decorating!

Trim ¼ inch from the short ends of the pound cake and discard. Cut cake into 1-inch-thick slices. Using a 1-inch to 1½-inch flower-shaped cookie cutter, cut 2 to 3 cakes from each slice of pound cake.

Divide frosting in small bowls and tint with assorted colors.

Frost the top of each flower cake with frosting and decorate with sprinkles, sugars, or candy decorations.

Sweet little cakes to share with a friend!

Sand Dollars

Ingredients List

¼ cup sugar

1 teaspoon cinnamon

1 tube refrigerator sugar
   cookie dough

1 egg white, slightly beaten

1 cup almond slivers

Makes about
2 dozen cookies

Eat these dollars,
don't spend them!

Let's get baking!

Preheat oven to 350 degrees F. Line two cookie sheets with foil and spray with nonstick cooking spray. Set aside.

Stir together sugar and cinnamon. Set aside.

Cut cookie dough into ¼-inch-thick slices and place 1 inch apart on prepared cookie sheets.

Lightly brush each cookie with egg white and then sprinkle evenly with sugar mixture.

Gently press 5 almond slivers in a star shape in the center of each cookie to look like the design of a sand dollar.

Bake cookies according to package directions. Remove from oven and cool 5 minutes on pan. Put cookies on wire rack to cool for another 10 minutes.

Hidden Treasure Cupcakes

Ingredients List

CUPCAKES

1 box strawberry cake mix

Apple juice

1 teaspoon vanilla extract

½ teaspoon almond extract

1 cup miniature marshmallows, white or colored

Let's get baking!

Preheat oven to 350 degrees F. Place twenty-four paper liners into muffin cups and spray the inside of each with nonstick cooking spray. Set aside.

Make cake mix according to package directions, substituting apple juice for water and adding vanilla and almond extracts.

Carefully fold marshmallows into batter and fill each muffin cup two-thirds full.

Bake for 15 to 20 minutes. Remove from oven and cool in pan on wire rack for 10 minutes.

Remove cupcakes from pan and cool another 15 minutes before frosting.

FROSTING

1 prepared container
   vanilla frosting

1 cup powdered sugar

½ teaspoon almond extract

Lime green paste
   food coloring

Makes 24 cupcakes

Let's get frosting!

Mix canned frosting, powdered sugar, almond extract, and food coloring in a medium-sized bowl.

Frost each cupcake generously with frosting.

A sweet hidden treasure awaits you!

Tiki Hut Fruit Tarts

Ingredients List

1 package refrigerator pie crust dough (2 pie crusts)

Flour for work surface

1 small box vanilla or white chocolate instant pudding

Milk

¼ teaspoon almond extract

2 drops orange food coloring

1 mango, peeled and cubed

2 kiwifruits, peeled and sliced

6 strawberries, thinly sliced

½ cup flaked coconut

Makes 12 tarts

Let's get baking!

Preheat oven to 350 degrees F. Spray a 12-cup muffin tin with nonstick cooking spray. Set aside.

Unfold 1 pie crust at a time and place on a lightly floured work surface. Turn pie crust over to make sure both sides are lightly coated with flour. Gently roll out pie crusts with a rolling pin.

Using a 3-inch flower-shaped or round cookie cutter, carefully cut out pieces of pie crust and put in each muffin cup. Continue until both pie crusts are used.

Prick bottoms of each crust with a fork. Chill crusts in muffin tin in refrigerator for 10 minutes before baking. Remove from refrigerator and bake for about 15 minutes, or until golden brown. Remove from oven and cool 5 minutes.

continued

While tart crusts are baking, make pudding according to package directions, adding almond extract and food coloring. Mix with a whisk until well blended. Cover and put in refrigerator until tart crusts have baked and cooled.

When ready to fill tarts, remove pudding from refrigerator. Spoon pudding into the bottom of each tart shell, filling each about three-fourths full. Top with mango cubes, kiwifruit slices, and strawberry slices. Sprinkle with coconut and chill in the refrigerator for 10 minutes, or until ready to serve. Best served the same day.

Fresh fruity tarts are fun!

Sea Queen Kabobs

Ingredients List

2 cups boiling water

2 large boxes blue gelatin

8 (6-inch) wooden skewers

16 to 20 gummy fish or
    Swedish fish candies

Makes 8

Let's get threading!

Stir boiling water into dry gelatin in a large bowl until completely dissolved. Pour carefully into a 9 x 13-inch pan. Refrigerate at least 3 hours, or until firm.

Remove pan from refrigerator and have an adult helper dip the bottom of pan in a sink full of warm water for about 15 to 20 seconds.

Place pan on counter and, using cookie cutters, cut gelatin into 1½-inch star, seashell, and fish shapes. Make sure the cookie cutter goes all the way through the gelatin to the bottom of the pan.

Lift cutout shapes from pan and carefully thread onto wooden skewers. Alternate gelatin shapes with gummy candies. Serve immediately.

This snack is queen of the sea!

Water Fairy Ice Pops

Ingredients List

1 (11-ounce) can Mandarin orange segments, drained

2 cups passion fruit or mango juice

12 to 18 cinnamon sticks

Makes 12–18 pops, depending on the size of the molds

Fairy magic frozen fun!

Let's get chilling!

Place 12 to 18 small soufflé cups or a decorative muffin pan onto a cookie sheet. Put 2 to 3 Mandarin orange segments into each cup.

Cut 12 to 18 (2-inch) squares of foil. Set aside.

Pour fruit juice into each cup about ¼ inch from the top. Place a small square of foil tightly over the opening of each cup. Have your adult assistant use a sharp knife to cut a very small slit (⅛ inch) into the center of each foil-covered cup.

Insert a cinnamon stick into each slit. This will be the ice pop's handle.

Place Popsicles in freezer for at least 2 hours. When ready to serve, carefully remove foil from each one and remove pops from cups. Serve immediately.

Banana Split Boats

Ingredients List

4 bananas with skins on, cut in half and then sliced open lengthwise

1 quart Neapolitan ice cream

Chocolate sauce

1 can whipped cream topping

Chocolate or rainbow sprinkles

1 (8-ounce) bottle maraschino cherries with stems, drained

Makes 8

Let's get scooping!

Place bananas on a cookie sheet. Put 1 scoop of ice cream in the center of each banana.

Top each scoop of ice cream with chocolate sauce, whipped cream, sprinkles, and a maraschino cherry. Place banana boats in freezer for 15 minutes. Remove from freezer and serve each on an individual plate.

Swim on over to your banana boat for a cool ice cream surprise!

Rainbow Fish Fudge

Ingredients List

¾ cup evaporated milk

1¾ cups sugar

½ teaspoon salt

1½ cups miniature
marshmallows

1½ cups semisweet
chocolate chips

1 teaspoon vanilla extract

½ cup rainbow sprinkles
or mini rainbow
chocolate chips

Makes about 24 pieces

Let's get stirring!

Lightly spray a 9-inch square pan with nonstick cooking spray. Set aside.

Combine evaporated milk with sugar in a medium saucepan. Bring to a boil; simmer for 5 minutes.

Remove from heat and stir in salt, marsh-mallows, chocolate chips, and vanilla. Stir until marshmallows have melted. Carefully pour mixture into prepared pan. Sprinkle top of fudge evenly with sprinkles or rain-bow chips. Chill in refrigerator for at least 2 hours before cutting.

Cut into fish shapes with a 2-inch cookie cutter and store covered in refrigerator until ready to serve.

Fun fishy fudge!

Seashell Candy

Ingredients List

½ pound vanilla candy coating
or vanilla almond bark

½ pound candy coating discs
in any pastel colors*

Makes 24 candies

*These can be found at any
craft store that carries Wilton
products.*

She sells seashell
candies!

Let's get melting!

Spray two 12-shell madeleine pans** with nonstick cooking spray. Set aside.

Melt each candy coating color in a different pan or container according to package directions. Cool for 2 to 3 minutes.

Put about 1 teaspoon vanilla candy coating into each mold. Spoon about 1 teaspoon colored candy coating on top of the vanilla and swirl with a Popsicle stick or toothpick.

Place pans in the refrigerator for 30 minutes. To remove candy from madeleine pans, turn over and tap on countertop. Any shells that remain in the pan may be carefully taken out by your adult assistant using the point of a sharp knife. Store candy shells covered in a cool place until ready to serve.

*** Madeleine pans have tiny molds that are shaped like seashells and may be found at gourmet gift stores or baking supply stores.*

Sea Maiden Sand Cups

Ingredients List

24 vanilla wafers, finely crushed

1 quart rainbow sherbet

Gummy fish or any chewy fruit sea creature candy

Makes 8

Let's get scooping!

Place vanilla wafers in a ziplock bag and seal shut. Place that bag in another ziplock bag and seal shut. Crush cookies with your hands until completely crumbled.

Place scoops of sherbet into serving cups. Fill cups within 1 inch from the top. Press sherbet down to flatten out top and cover each with equal amounts of cookie crumb mixture. Garnish with gummy fish or sea creature candy.

A sea maiden's favorite dessert!

Collect them all!

With a degree in elementary education and a passion for cooking, *Barbara Beery* is the quintessential cooking instructor for kids. Barbara founded Batter Up Kids in 1991 to offer interactive classes that focus on teaching kids to cook, healthier eating options, and fun. Barbara is a best-selling cookbook author, entrepreneur, and experienced spokesperson; she is always looking to stir up more kid-friendly opportunities in the kitchen.

www.gibbs-smith.com

www.batterupkids.com

www.kidscookingshop.com